The Silver Hunters

Written by Zoë Clarke
Illustrated by Lidia Fernandez

Collins

Meet the silver hunters

Kit

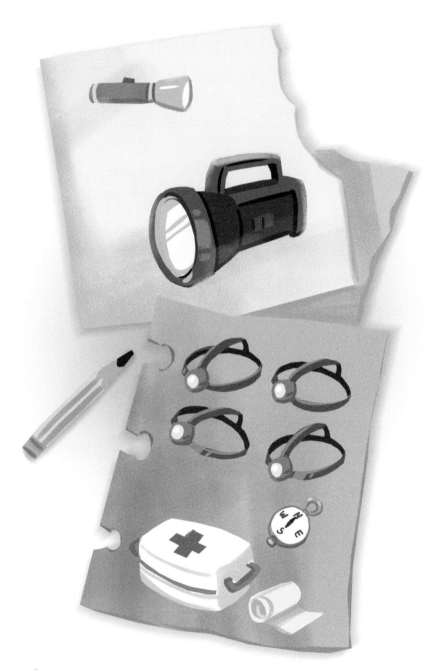

Finn has a torn map.

silver

tunnel

Thorn Wood

8

They sail down the river near Thorn Wood.

They get to the hidden tunnel.

They push sharp rocks.

They see chinks of light!

18

Hidden silver

21

Silver hunt

🐾 Review: After reading 🐾

Use your assessment from hearing the children read to choose any GPCs, words or tricky words that need additional practice.

Read 1: Decoding

- Focus on the words with long vowels, and longer words.
  - o Point to these words on pages 10 and 11 for the children to read. Ask: Can you point to the digraphs or trigraphs?

sail (*ai*)	**down** (*ow*)	**river** (*er*)	**near** (*ear*)
thorn (*or*)	**look** (*oo*)	**eels** (*ee*)	

- Remind the children that they can read the words in chunks at first. Then challenge them to read the words without chunking them up. Say: Can you read the words fluently? Try to read them in one go.

silver	**hidden**	**tunnel**	**hunters**

Read 2: Prosody

- Encourage the children to read pages 16 and 17 with expression.
- Point out the exclamation marks and remind them that this means we need to read with extra expression. For each page, ask: What emotion should we show in our voice? (e.g. *excitement, then surprise*)

Read 3: Comprehension

- Encourage the children to talk about adventure stories that involve a hunt for something.
- Ask: In this story, why is the tear in the map important? (*a missing bit of the map made the children think there was silver in the tunnel*) If necessary, point to the picture on page 19, and ask: Was there ever silver in the tunnel? (*no, there are only silver fish*)
- Turn to page 16 and point to **chinks**. Discuss its meaning in context, asking: What would "chinks of light" be like? (e.g. *tiny patches of light; light coming through tiny holes*)
- Turn to pages 22 and 23, and focus on each picture to discuss what extra exciting events could have happened along the way. Prompt with questions, such as:
  - o What might the eels have turned out to be? (e.g. *monsters*) How did the children escape? (*they threw their sandwiches in the river for the eels to eat*)
  - o What if there was a rock slide? Who comes to help them? (e.g. *a giant; a mountaineer*)
- Bonus content: Using pages 2 to 5 for names and their kit, ask the children to think up a new adventure in which the children find one of the types of silver on pages 20 and 21.